ORNITHOMIMUS

by Laura Alden
illustrated by Ching

THE CHILD'S WORLD

MANKATO, MN

*Grateful appreciation is expressed to
Bret S. Beall, Research Consultant,
Field Museum of Natural History, Chicago,
Illinois, who reviewed this book to
insure its accuracy.*

Library of Congress Cataloging in Publication Data

Alden, Laura, 1955-
  Ornithomimus / by Laura Alden ; illustrated by Ching.
    p. cm. — (Dinosaur books)
  Summary: Presents facts and theories about the physical
characteristics and behavior of the Ornithomimus.
  ISBN 0-89565-630-2 (lib. bdg.)
  1. Ornithomimus—Juvenile literature.   [1. Ornithomimus.
2. Dinosaurs.]   I. Ching, ill.   II. Title.   III. Series: Riehecky,
Janet, 1953-   Dinosaur books.
QE862.S3A433   1990
567.9'7—dc20   90-2597
                                                         CIP
                                                         AC

1 2 3 4 5 6 7 8 9 10 11 12 R 98 97 96 95 94 93 92 91

ORNITHOMIMUS

Long ago, dinosaurs walked on the earth. They ran and swam on it too . . .

4

usually in search of something to eat!

There were some dinosaurs that had to dash in and steal their food. They liked to eat and run.

There were heavy, spiny dinosaurs that lumbered along until they spied some plants to munch on. They grazed like cows, though they didn't look anything like cows!

Then there were the meat eaters that liked the taste of other dinosaurs. Some of these were as big as a bus and shook the earth with each step they took.

The plant-eating dinosaurs soon learned they must run faster than these dinosaurs—or get eaten!

One dinosaur that stayed a step ahead of all the others was the Ornithomimus (or-nith-oh-MIME-us), whose name means "bird mimic." With its long legs, long neck, and small head, it looked like an ostrich. It also ran like an ostrich. Some scientists think the Ornithomimus could run as fast as fifty miles per hour. That would make the Ornithomimus one of the fastest dinosaurs ever discovered.

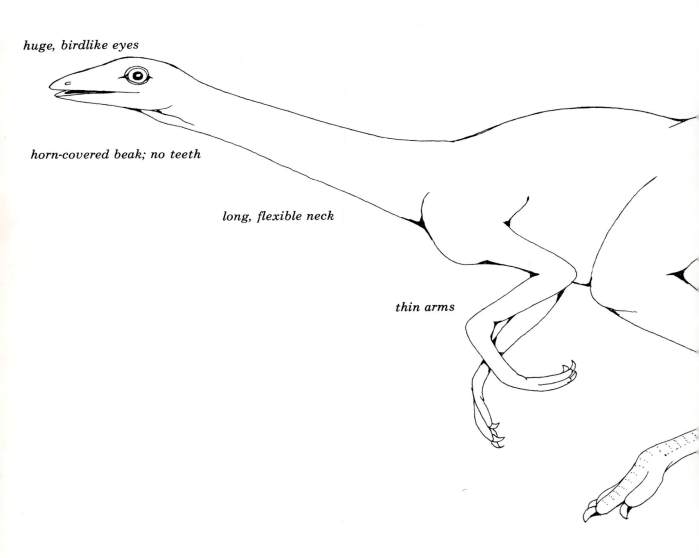

huge, birdlike eyes

horn-covered beak; no teeth

long, flexible neck

thin arms

Ornithomimus had a runner's body. Its legs were long and strong, made for running. And it could stretch its neck and tail into a straight line to make fast getaways.

very long tail

powerful hind legs

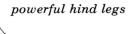

long feet

Though it had a small, light head, the Or-nithomimus had a large brain. Not only could this dinosaur outrun its enemies, it could outsmart them too!

This "ostrich" dinosaur grew to be thirteen feet long and as tall as a very tall basketball player—about seven feet. But instead of shooting baskets, the Ornithomimus used its height, along with its arms and claws, to reach the leaves and fruit on tall trees.

Most scientists think the Ornithomimus was not a picky eater. They think it ate both plants and small animals. That could be why this dinosaur lived for five million years—until the end of the age of dinosaurs.

It may not have been picky, but the Ornithomimus did have to work hard at
eating. For one thing, it had no teeth! It
had to use its beak to grab bites of fruit,
leaves, insects, or lizards. And it couldn't
chew, so it swallowed the chunks
whole—just as birds do.

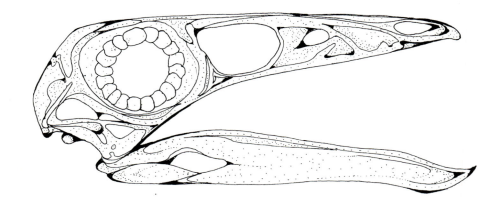

The Ornithomimus could twist its neck about like a bird to pick up seeds or fruit from the ground. But it did not soar through the air, catching insects. The Ornithomimus had no wings, and it could not fly. Of course, it didn't need to fly when it could run like the wind.

The Ornithomimus could also use its long, strong claws to get food. It could rip apart rotten logs or scrape away brush to look for a few good insects. It could even dig through the sand to uncover nests of dinosaur eggs. If it found some eggs, it could use its sharp beak to break them open and then gobble the tasty insides.

Stop, thief! Of course, other dinosaurs did not like having their eggs stolen. The Ornithomimus ran into big trouble (and big horns!) if it was caught stealing. So it used its keen eyes to watch for other dinosaurs. That helped the Ornithomimus stay out of trouble, at least some of the time.

But what did the Ornithomimus do if it was surprised by an enemy? Some scientists think it gave the enemy an "ostrich kick." An ostrich can kill a lion with its strong kick.

But some enemies were much bigger than a lion. They wouldn't have been scared of being kicked. So the best thing the Ornithomimus could do to protect itself was run. Head up! Tail back! The Ornithomimus would soon be out of reach —and out of sight.

Scientists don't know much about the family life of the Ornithomimus. Some have wondered if it had its babies alive, but most think it laid eggs as many other dinosaurs did. The Ornithomimus may have scooped out a nest in the ground—and then guarded that nest against other egg thieves!

Scientists think the Ornithomimus was a good parent. They believe it brought food to its babies and protected them from danger. When the babies got old enough to travel, many Ornithomimus probably traveled together in herds with the babies in the center for more protection.

Scientists think the herds traveled far and wide. They picture them running through flat, open areas and visiting nearby swamps and forests to find food.

Scientists don't know why the Ornithomimus died out. They became extinct
millions of years ago along with all the
other dinosaurs.

Many scientists think the end of the
dinosaur age came after a big asteroid hit

the earth. Such a collision might have made huge clouds of dust. If the clouds blocked out the sun for years or even months, the plants would all have died, and new ones wouldn't have grown. Slowly, the dinosaurs would have starved.

Some scientists think the dinosaurs died because of a disease. Still others believe the earth's weather changed and became too cold for dinosaurs.

The reason for the death of the dinosaurs may always be a mystery. But we do know many things about them: how they looked, ate, and lived. And we know how to picture the Ornithomimus—it was always on the run!

Dinosaur Fun

When a kind of plant or animal, such as the dinosaur, becomes extinct, that means it is gone forever. In modern times, many, many plants and animals have become extinct. Many more are endangered. That means they will become extinct if they are not protected.

What can you do to help protect endangered animals? The first step is to learn about them. Look for information about endangered animals in newspapers, magazines, and books. Ask your librarian to help you find out about groups that work to protect endangered animals, such as the World Wildlife Fund. You can also write to the United States Fish and Wildlife Service for information. Their address is:

United States Fish and Wildlife Service
Publications Unit
130 Arlington Square Building
18th and C Streets NW
Washington, D.C. 20240